OUR GALAXY AND BEYOND

JUPITER

By Charnan Simon

The Child's World

Published in the United States of America by The Child's World®
P.O. Box 326, Chanhassen, MN 55317-0326
800-599-READ
www.childsworld.com

Content Adviser:
Michelle Nichols,
Lead Educator for
Informal Programs,
Adler Planetarium
& Astronomy
Museum, Chicago,
Illinois

Photo Credits: Cover: NASA/JPL/Caltech; Bettmann/Corbis: 7, 9; Corbis: 5, 6 (Araldo de Luca), 19 (Rykoff Collection), 25; Corbis Sygma: 13; NASA/JPL/Caltech: 14, 15, 16, 20, 21, 23, 24 (Arizona State University), 27, 31; NASA/JPL/Caltech/University of Arizona: 11, 17, 22.

The Child's World®: Mary Berendes, Publishing Director
Editorial Directions, Inc.: E. Russell Primm, Editorial Director; Dana Rau, Line Editor; Elizabeth K. Martin, Assistant Editor; Olivia Nellums, Editorial Assistant; Susan Hindman, Copy Editor; Susan Ashley, Proofreader; Kevin Cunningham, Peter Garnham, Chris Simms, Fact Checkers; Tim Griffin/IndexServ, Indexer; Cian Loughlin O'Day, Photo Researcher; Linda S. Koutris, Photo Selector

Library of Congress Cataloging-in-Publication Data
Simon, Charnan.
 Jupiter / by Charnan Simon.
   p. cm. — (Our galaxy and beyond)
Includes index.
Contents: Discovering Jupiter—An atmosphere with attitude—Inside Jupiter—Fifty-two moons—A magnificent magnet—How did Jupiter form?
 ISBN 1-59296-049-9 (lib. bdg. : alk. paper)
 1. Jupiter (Planet)—Juvenile literature. [1. Jupiter (Planet)] I. Title. II. Series.
 QB661.S584 2004
 523.45—dc21   2003008038

TABLE OF CONTENTS

CHAPTER ONE

DISCOVERING JUPITER

Jupiter is the largest planet in our solar system. It is twice as large as all eight of the other planets, plus all the **comets, asteroids,** and moons put together. If Jupiter were hollow, more than 1,300 Earths would fit inside!

A solar system is made up of a star, like our Sun; the planets, asteroids, and comets that orbit, or go around, it; and the moons that orbit the planets. Jupiter is like a mini-solar system. It is huge and hot. It is surrounded by at least 61 moons that orbit Jupiter the same way the planets orbit the Sun.

Jupiter is the fifth planet from the Sun. It moves around the Sun in a path shaped almost like a circle, but not quite. This means that its distance from the Sun is not always the same. After Venus, Jupiter

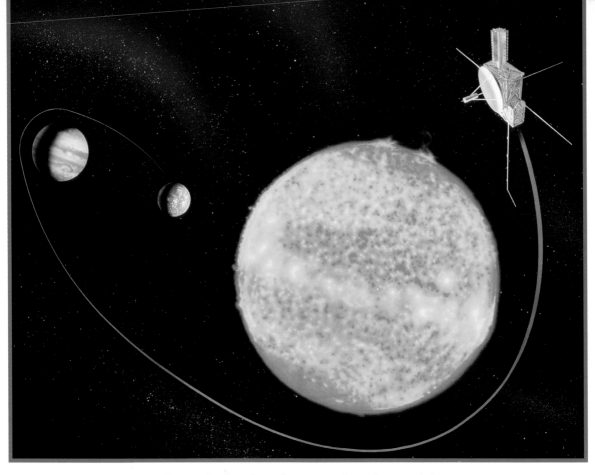

A satellite tracks the orbits of Jupiter and Earth around the Sun.

is the second brightest planet in the night sky. People have been

observing this giant for thousands of years. In 364 B.C., a Chinese

astronomer named Gan De may have been the first person to

see Jupiter's moons. He described seeing an object that modern

astronomers think was Ganymede, Jupiter's largest moon. Years later,

the ancient Romans admired the planet's brightness from the other

Jupiter was the most powerful of all the Roman gods. The planet Jupiter was named after him because of its great size.

side of Earth. They named it Jupiter, after their most important god.

In 1610, the famous Italian astronomer Galileo became the first person to see Jupiter through a **telescope.** Galileo was surprised to also see four small, bright objects circling Jupiter. He had discovered the largest of Jupiter's many moons. Today, we call these four moons the Galilean moons.

Soon, other astronomers looked at Jupiter through their telescopes. By 1660, they had found what looked like dark belts circling the planet. In 1664, astronomers saw a huge, reddish spot on Jupiter's southern half.

Over time, bigger and better telescopes have been built. Many spacecraft have helped modern scientists study Jupiter. Astronomers

*The things Galileo discovered simply by looking through his telescope
dramatically changed the way people thought about the universe.
Many of his ideas proved correct and have lasted through time.*

continue to find more moons around Jupiter. They have also dis-

covered that the dark belts are really huge, swirling clouds of gas.

In 1972, the *Pioneer 10* spacecraft was launched. It flew within

80,000 miles (130,000 kilometers) of Jupiter. In 1974, *Pioneer 11*

flew even closer, within 25,000 miles (40,233 km) of the planet.

These spacecraft sent back the first close-up pictures of Jupiter. They showed that the huge red spot was really a gigantic hurricane-like storm that has been raging for more than 300 years.

The *Voyager 1* and *Voyager 2* spacecraft followed in 1977. By 1979, they had flown close enough to find a real surprise. Jupiter has rings around it! These rings are made of tiny chunks of ice and dust. They aren't nearly as large or bright as Saturn's rings, but scientists were excited by the new discovery.

Finally, on October 18, 1989, the *Galileo* spacecraft set out on a **mission** to study Jupiter. Part of the spacecraft, called the orbiter, circled Jupiter. It studied the planet and its many moons. *Galileo* sent back pictures of Jupiter that were a hundred times clearer than any seen before. Scientists are still learning about Jupiter from information sent back to Earth by the *Galileo* spacecraft.

NICOLAUS COPERNICUS

The Polish astronomer Nicolaus Copernicus discovered much about Jupiter and the solar system. He lived from 1473 to 1543, decades before Galileo observed the planets through his telescope. Copernicus is considered the father of modern astronomy.

Five hundred years ago, when Copernicus was alive, people thought that the Sun and all the planets orbited Earth. But Copernicus did not agree. He came up with a **theory** that explained how Earth and the solar system worked. One part of his theory explained that Earth and the other planets orbit the Sun.

Using mathematics, Copernicus decided that some planets must take longer to orbit the Sun than others. By watching and studying Jupiter, he figured out that it takes Jupiter almost 12 Earth-years to orbit the Sun.

At first, not everyone accepted the new theory, because it went against everything they believed about the universe. But years after Copernicus's death, Galileo helped prove that parts of his theory were correct. His discovery of four moons orbiting Jupiter showed that not everything revolved around Earth.

CHAPTER TWO

JUPITER'S ATMOSPHERE

An atmosphere is the layer of gases that surrounds a planet. Much of what we know about the atmosphere of Jupiter was gathered by the *Galileo* spacecraft. In 1995, the *Galileo* orbiter released a **probe** that parachuted into Jupiter's clouds. For nearly an hour, this probe was battered by violent winds as it fell through Jupiter's hot, heavy atmosphere. It recorded information about clouds, lightning, and gases in the atmosphere. It did all this in only 59 minutes, before it was destroyed by the heat and pressure of Jupiter's atmosphere. But the information it was able to collect has been enormously helpful to scientists.

Earth's atmosphere is mostly nitrogen and oxygen. This is a perfect atmosphere for people and animals to breathe. Jupiter's atmosphere, however, is mostly hydrogen and helium. It also has smaller amounts of other gases, such as methane, ammonia, and sulfur. These gases are poisonous to human beings.

When you look at Jupiter through a telescope, it looks striped. The entire planet is circled by red, orange, tan, yellow, white, and purple bands. These bands are clouds that are hundreds of miles

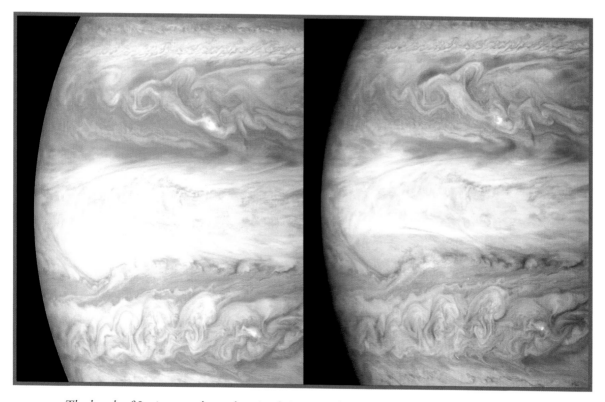

The bands of Jupiter are shown here in their true colors on the left and exaggerated color on the right. Each band is a different direction of cloud motion.

deep. The lighter-colored clouds are called zones. The darker ones are known as belts.

At the top of the clouds, it is colder than anywhere on Earth. Temperatures are as low as –250° Fahrenheit (–157° Celsius). But if you were to drop 600 miles (966 km) beneath the clouds, the temperature reaches 6,000° F (3,315° C). The core, or center, of Jupiter is deeper still and is an amazing 54,000° F (30,000° C).

Winds rage on Jupiter. The *Galileo* probe measured winds blowing 450 miles (724 km) per hour. That is more than twice as fast as even the wildest hurricane on Earth. The winds push the bands of clouds around the planet. They cause storms that last for weeks, months, or even years. These storms show up in the clouds as beautiful swirls and streaks. Jupiter is an exciting planet to look at through a telescope.

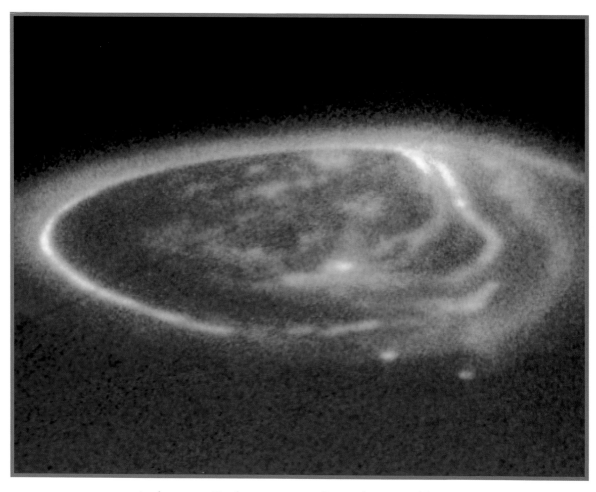

A telescope on Earth captures one of Jupiter's many wild storms.

What causes Jupiter's winds and wild storms? They are partly a result of the way Jupiter rotates, or turns, on its axis. The axis is an imaginary line between the top and bottom of a planet, called its poles. Every planet rotates on its axis. It takes Earth 24 hours, or one day, to rotate once. Jupiter is much, much larger than Earth.

Scientists created this 3-D diagram of the cloud layers on Jupiter near its equator from information they received from the Galileo *spacecraft.*

But it spins much, much faster. It only takes Jupiter about 10 hours to turn around once on its axis. This rapid spinning causes the planet's incredibly fast winds.

Another reason for Jupiter's storms is its heat. Have you ever watched steam rising from a hot cup of tea? The heat escaping from Jupiter's super-hot center rises in the same way. Jupiter's spinning pushes this heat into wild storms.

The circular shape of these huge spots on Jupiter tell scientists that they are storms.

THE GREAT RED SPOT

One storm has been raging on Jupiter for more than 300 years! In 1664, a British scientist named Robert Hooke noticed a large, reddish spot on the southern part of Jupiter. In the 1970s, the *Pioneer* spacecraft confirmed that this area, known as the Great Red Spot, was a storm much like an enormous hurricane. The Great Red Spot measures 8,000 miles (13,000 km) high and 18,000 miles (29,000 km) long. That's big enough to hold almost three Earths! But scientists say it is shrinking. Today, the spot is only about half as big as it was 100 years ago. The planet Neptune also has large spots on its surface, but they are all smaller and younger than the mysterious Great Red Spot of Jupiter.

CHAPTER THREE

WHAT JUPITER IS MADE OF

Jupiter is called a gas giant. Like Saturn, Uranus, and Neptune, Jupiter is a huge planet made up mostly of gases. Jupiter doesn't have a rocky crust, or surface, like Earth, though it does have a solid center.

The outermost layer of Jupiter is a constantly swirling layer of clouds. Little or no sunlight can get through these clouds. Under them, massive lightning storms flash in the sky. Farther beneath the

Looking at the surface of Jupiter, a person might think that it is solid and smooth. However, underneath its many layers of storms, no one really knows where the inner core of Jupiter is.

clouds is an ocean of liquid hydrogen. No one knows for sure, but scientists think this ocean might be 10,000 miles (16,000 km) deep! Scientists also think there is probably a core of rock and ice at the center of Jupiter that is 10 to 20 times as large as Earth.

On the surface of Earth, there is about 2,000 pounds (907 kilograms) of air pressing down on you. This is called air pressure. We do not feel air pressure on Earth because we are used to it. However, the air pressure on Jupiter is enormous. It is probably 30 million times greater than the pressure on Earth's surface! Even if people could stand the heat, the poisonous gases, and the raging winds, they would be crushed by Jupiter's air pressure. This is what happened with the *Galileo* probe. Still, scientists wonder if there might be some form of life in Jupiter's atmosphere. If there is, it would be very different from anything we know on Earth.

Much of what we know about Jupiter's atmosphere comes from information sent back to Earth from spaceships. The Space Age began in 1957, when the Soviet Union (now Russia) launched the unmanned spacecraft *Sputnik I.* An unmanned spacecraft carries only machines, not people. A month later, the Soviet Union followed with *Sputnik II,* which carried a dog named Laika into space. In 1969, the first astronauts from the United States landed on the Moon.

Space travel has greatly improved since the days of *Sputnik.* But the other planets in our solar system are too far away for astronauts to travel to them. Instead, scientists send probes to explore the far reaches of space. Probes don't carry people, but they do carry cameras and other scientific instruments.

Some probes fly past planets, while others orbit or even land on them. Some go on one-way journeys, and some bring samples and information back to Earth. The *Galileo* orbiter ended its mission by crashing into Jupiter in September 2003. *Pioneer 10* has already passed Jupiter and can no longer send information back to Earth. It has left our solar system and is traveling far beyond the reach of Earth's radios.

CHAPTER FOUR

A MAGNIFICENT MAGNET

Jupiter is like an enormous magnet whirling around in space.

Scientists think that deep inside Jupiter is a huge layer of hot, liquid

metallic hydrogen. Hydrogen gas becomes liquid metallic hydrogen

only at very high pressure, such as the pressure found on Jupiter.

Jupiter's strong magnetic field holds space dust in the form of rings
in orbit around its outer layer of storms.

While Jupiter spins, the motion makes this liquid metallic hydrogen act like a magnet.

As a magnet, Jupiter has its own magnetic field. A magnetic field is the area where a mag-

Many moons are caught in Jupiter's extremely strong magnetic field. Three of the most well-known of these, seen here, are Callisto, Io, and Europa, from left to right.

net's force can be felt. It is the area where a magnet works. Have you ever used a magnet to make steel paper clips "jump" off a table? They attach themselves to the magnet because they are inside the magnetic field. If you hold the magnet too far away, the paper clips will not move. They are outside the magnetic field.

The magnetic field around a planet is called its magnetosphere. Jupiter has the largest magnetosphere in the solar system. It reaches almost a million miles into space.

CHAPTER FIVE

JUPITER'S MANY MOONS

Many more moons have been discovered circling Jupiter since the days of Galileo. As recently as February 2003, six new moons were spotted. So far, the total has reached 61 moons—more than any other planet in the solar system.

The four Galilean moons are Jupiter's largest. Thanks to information returned to Earth by *Voyager* and other spacecraft, we know quite a lot about these moons.

Ganymede is the largest moon in the solar system. It is larger than the planets Pluto and Mercury. Ganymede is also the only moon

Jupiter's moon Io is shown here as it would appear to the human eye. Scientists observe Io's many volcanoes as can be seen in this image.

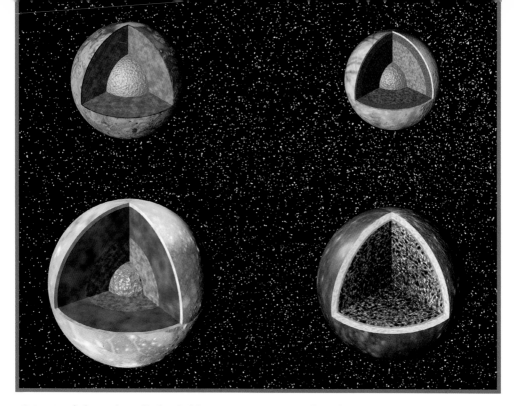

Scientists believe that all the Galilean moons except Callisto have metallic cores. They think Ganymede and Europa have layers of water in between layers of rock core and crust.

in the solar system that has its own magnetic field. Ganymede's magnetic field extends for miles out into space.

Io has more active **volcanoes** than any other planet or moon in the solar system. In 1979, *Voyager 1* took pictures of eight volcanoes erupting at the same time on Io! These volcanoes erupt liquid sulfur and send clouds of sulfur gas hundreds of miles into space.

This view of the moon Europa's surface gives scientists evidence that water may have existed on Europa recently.

Callisto is covered with craters. Scientists think Callisto's landscape may be the oldest in the solar system. The craters are bowl-shaped holes that were caused by **meteorites** striking the moon billions of years ago.

Europa is the smallest of the Galilean moons. It looks smooth and white. It doesn't have high mountains or rocky craters like Earth's Moon. Instead, Europa is covered by a vast sheet of ice. Scientists think there may be a liquid water ocean beneath this frozen surface.

Astronomers are still discovering moons orbiting Jupiter. Watch out for new moon discoveries. By the time you read this book, Jupiter may have up to 100 moons!

SHOEMAKER-LEVY 9

A comet is an object made of rocks and frozen gas, followed by a tail of dust and ice. Usually comets orbit the Sun in a long, slow path. However, some comets circle between the Sun and Jupiter in a short, quick path. This is because Jupiter is so large that it can attract comets with its strong gravity, the force that pulls one object toward another. In 1993, one such comet, named Shoemaker-Levy 9, was discovered. This comet had been broken into smaller pieces by Jupiter's gravity. When astronomers figured out the comet's orbit, they found that the pieces of the comet would soon crash into Jupiter.

Some people called it the astronomical event of the century. Over one week in July 1994, the pieces of Comet Shoemaker-Levy 9 crashed through Jupiter's atmosphere. A comet usually leaves a crater when it hits the surface of a planet or a moon. But the pieces of this comet probably burned up in Jupiter's atmosphere before they could get too far. They created huge explosions that made dark marks appear in Jupiter's cloud cover. Even backyard stargazers with small telescopes could see the marks. These patches spread into a band that circled Jupiter for more than a year before fading away.

CHAPTER SIX

HOW JUPITER MAY HAVE FORMED

Scientists may never know exactly how the Sun and the planets formed, but they do have a theory. Nearly five billion years ago, our solar system formed from a large cloud of gas and dust in space. This cloud began to spin and collapse. At the very center of the cloud, the Sun formed. Away from the center, particles, or tiny pieces, of dust and gas clumped together to form chunks. Some chunks eventually formed planets. Those closest to the Sun were made mostly of rock and metal. These rocky planets are Mercury, Venus, Earth, and Mars.

Farther from the Sun, where it was cooler, solid particles and pieces of ice came together to form much larger rocky bodies. At the same time, the newly formed Sun was blowing gas and dust into the outer solar system. The bodies that would become Jupiter and Saturn grew large enough to pull in a lot of that gas and dust with their gravity. That gas and dust made Jupiter the enormous gas giant that we see today.

Astronomers still have many questions about Jupiter and how it formed. They hope that the information gathered by future spacecraft will help them unlock some the secrets of this mysterious giant.

· Jupiter is so large that it dwarfs its four Galilean moons. But Europa, the smallest of the four, is about the size of Earth. That means all of these moons are big enough to be planets themselves. Imagine how big Jupiter is!

Glossary

asteroids (ASS-tuh-royds) Asteroids are rocky objects that orbit the Sun.

astronomer (uh-STRAW-nuh-mer) An astronomer is a scientist who studies space and the stars and planets.

comets (KOM-its) Comets are bright objects followed by a tail of dust and ice that orbits the Sun in a long, slow path.

meteorites (MEE-tee-uh-rites) Meteorites are rocky, metallic objects from space that hit the surface of a planet or moon.

mission (MISH-uhn) A mission is a special task or a purpose.

probe (PROBE) A probe is a machine or tool that explores something.

telescope (TEL-uh-skope) A telescope is an instrument used to study things that are far away, such as stars and planets, by making them seem larger and closer.

theory (THEE-uh-ree) A theory is an idea that explains how or why something may have happened or describes how something works.

volcanoes (vol-KAY-nose) Volcanoes are mountains that contain an opening in the surface of a planet. When a volcano erupts, melted rock from pools of magma below the surface spews from the top.

Did You Know?

▸ Some of Jupiter's outer moons are possibly asteroids that have been captured by the giant planet's gravity.

▸ Jupiter's ring is really three rings. Pictures from the *Voyager* spacecraft show a main center ring, an inner ring called a halo, and a very fine, faint outer ring.

▸ Most of the volcanoes on Io are named after fire gods. One, Loki, is named for a Norwegian god of mischief.

- In 1665, a French astronomer named Jean Dominique Cassini became the first person to figure out that it takes Jupiter just under 10 hours to rotate once on its axis.

- Jupiter gives off twice as much heat as it receives from the Sun. Jupiter was hot when it was formed—and it is still hot today.

Fast Facts

Diameter: 88,846 miles (142,984 km)

Atmosphere: hydrogen, helium, methane, ammonia, sulfur

Time to orbit the Sun (one Jupiter-year): 11.9 Earth-years

Time to turn on axis (one Jupiter-day): 9 hours, 51 minutes

Shortest distance from the Sun: 460 million miles (741 million km)

Greatest distance from the Sun: 507 million miles (816 million km)

Shortest distance from Earth: 366 million miles (589 million km)

Greatest distance from Earth: 602 million miles (968 million km)

Surface gravity: 2.6 that of Earth. If you weighed 80 pounds (36 kg) on Earth, you would weigh about 208 pounds (94 kg) on Jupiter.

Temperature range: 54,000° F (30,000° C) at core; −250° F (−157° C) at top of clouds; about 6,000° F (3,315° C) 600 miles (966 km) beneath tops of clouds

Number of known moons: 61

How to Learn More about Jupiter

At the Library

Asimov, Isaac, and Richard Hantula. *Jupiter.* Milwaukee: Gareth Stevens, 2002.

Cole, Michael. *Galileo Spacecraft: Mission to Jupiter.* Springfield, N.J.: Enslow, 1999.

Cole, Michael. *Jupiter: The Fifth Planet.* Springfield, N.J.: Enslow, 2001.

Haugen, David M. *Jupiter.* San Diego: Kidhaven Press, 2002.

Kerrod, Robin. *The Far Planets.* Austin, Tex.: Raintree Steck-Vaughn, 2002.

Miller, Ron. *Jupiter.* Brookfield, Conn.: Twenty-First Century Books, 2002.

Schwabacher, Martin. *Jupiter.* New York: Benchmark Books, 2001.

Simon, Seymour. *Destination: Jupiter.* New York: Morrow Junior Books, 1998.

Sparrow, Giles. *Jupiter.* Chicago: Heinemann Library, 2001.

On the Web

Visit our home page for lots of links about Jupiter:
http://www.childsworld.com/links.html
Note to Parents, Teachers, and Librarians: We routinely verify our Web links to
make sure they're safe, active sites—so encourage your readers to check them out!

Through the Mail or by Phone

ADLER PLANETARIUM AND ASTRONOMY MUSEUM
1300 South Lake Shore Drive
Chicago, IL 60605-2403
312/922-STAR

NATIONAL AIR AND SPACE MUSEUM
7th and Independence Avenue, S.W.
Washington, DC 20560
202/357-2700

ROSE CENTER FOR EARTH AND SPACE AMERICAN MUSEUM OF NATURAL HISTORY
Central Park West at 79th Street
New York, NY 10024-5192
212/769-5100

The Sun

Mercury

Venus

Earth

Mars

Jupiter

Saturn

Uranus

Neptune

Pluto

The solar system

Index

About the Author

Charnan Simon has a B.A. in English literature from Carleton College and an M.A. in English literature from the University of Chicago. She began her publishing career in Boston, in the children's book division of Little, Brown and Company. She also spent six years as an editor at *Cricket* magazine before becoming a full-time author. Simon has written more than 40 books for kids, and numerous magazine stories and articles. In addition to writing and freelance editing, she is also a contributing editor for *Click* magazine. Simon lives in Madison, Wisconsin, with her husband Tom, their daughters, Ariel and Hana, Sam the dog, and Lily and Luna the cats.